Keynsham Church, 1879.

The Changing Face of
Keynsham

IN OLD PHOTOGRAPHS

BARBARA LOWE *and*
MARGARET WHITEHEAD
ON BEHALF OF
KEYNSHAM & SALTFORD
LOCAL HISTORY SOCIETY

Alan Sutton Publishing Limited
Phoenix Mill · Far Thrupp · Stroud
Gloucestershire

First Published 1994

British Library Cataloguing in Publication Data.
A catalogue record for this book is available from
the British Library.

ISBN 0-7509-0727-4

Typeset in 9/10 Sabon.
Typesetting and origination by
Alan Sutton Publishing Limited.
Printed in Great Britain by
Ebenezer Baylis, Worcester.

Contents

Samson subduing the lion. One of the beautifully detailed Romanesque embossed keystones rescued from the bypass cutting below Abbey Meade. Some people think he represents David, not Samson.

Introduction

The geographical position of Keynsham, close to the confluence of the rivers Chew and Avon, with rich pastures, abundant woodland and limestone outcrops, has made it attractive to settlers from early times. Prehistoric man passed through, leaving hand axes and flint tools. The Romans constructed several villas in the area, with a substantial settlement on the Hams (probably Trajectus). The largest Roman house was discovered under Keynsham Cemetery and portions may still exist under the old A4 nearby. The construction of Fry's factory in the 1920s revealed a small villa, burial-ground and a well. 'A temple is thought to have been nearby. In 1991 the levelling of playing fields exposed part of a Roman settlement and road. Local archaeologists are still voluntarily rescuing artefacts in spoil from the settlement. The location of Keynsham's Saxon minster is not yet known, but Saxon artefacts and fragments of carved stone have been recovered.

The remains of the once large, rich and important abbey have been plundered piecemeal since 1539, with the construction of Keynsham bypass between 1961 and 1966 dealing the final blow. Only the dedicated voluntary work of members of Bristol Folk House Archaeological Society prevented the whole abbey being swept away without knowledge even of its ground-plan. Exquisite Romanesque and later sculpture, tiles and other artefacts were rescued. Some foundation walling may still survive below Memorial Park.

The Dissolution of the Monasteries in 1539 changed the underlying structure of the town, removing the industry and security which the abbey had provided for almost four hundred years. The considerable lands of the manor and hundreds were eventually split up and sold to absentee landlords. The abundance of water, supporting several mills, ensured the continuation of milling industries such as corn grinding, fulling, brass making and working, steel making, and the processing of flax and dyewoods.

The influence of the Quaker, Methodist and Baptist movements was felt here, and from the eighteenth century there was a constant stream of private schools offering good education. The coming of the railway in the mid-nineteenth century affected river and road transport and caused the running down of coaching inns like the Talbot, New Inn, Lamb & Lark and the Crown. From the 1920s, J.S. Fry & Sons' factory gave much needed employment to the area.

Post-war Keynsham underwent a much more rapid change than before. The frenzy of demolition and redevelopment swept away many architectural gems and aesthetically pleasing vistas. Gradually the family living-quarters behind or over the shops were replaced with offices and storerooms. Small family businesses, established over several lifetimes, were squeezed out by branches of large national companies, reducing our High Street to a haven for banks, building societies and charity shops.

However, Keynsham is still a grand place in which to live!

Keynsham Market, *c.* 1933. Cooper & Tanner ran the market east of the Talbot along Bath Road, from 1923 until December 1975.

SECTION ONE
Down with the Old

Demolition of the solid Victorian houses in The Park in 1964 for the bypass cutting.

Keynsham railway station, *c.* 1907, looking towards Saltford. The main building housed Station Master Samuel Lambert and once had decorative stone squirrels and other animals on its roof. The original Brunel footbridge and signal-box are seen beyond. In 1840 an 'Orpheus' Roman mosaic pavement, discovered while cutting the railway line at Newton St Loe, was relaid in the waiting room of Keynsham station until taken to Bristol Museum in 1851.

A later picture showing the footbridge (roofed by 1919) which was removed in 1970 and is now over the Totnes to Buckfastleigh private line.

Keynsham & Somerdale station, *c.* 1960, with a steam train coming from Bristol. Notice how well kept the station was then.

Early morning commuters of 1960, leaving the station on their way to work at Fry's chocolate factory. Notice the lollipop man to see them safely across the perilous Willsbridge Road.

The neatly maintained booking office and waiting room, with an attractive canopy, *c*. 1953.

The last Keynsham Station Master, Norman Robert Bartrum, 1952–65. On the left the line branches to Fry's Somerdale factory.

The destruction of Keynsham station in 1970.

The bare station in 1979. Few trains stopped here; there was no ticket office or footbridge and just canopies for shelter. Public demand has since resulted in an improved train service, another footbridge and an early morning ticket office.

The gatehouse and weighbridge (destroyed in the spring of 1994) at the main entrance to Fry's factory. The factory also served as a museum for the Roman artefacts from Keynsham Cemetery villa and the small villa found when Fry's factory was being constructed, 1924–5. In 1988 the Keynsham artefacts were boxed and transferred to storage rooms in Keynsham Town Hall.

Workers leaving Fry's on foot, bicycle and bus, c. 1933. Workers commuted from miles around and special buses and trains ran for them. Keynsham station became Keynsham & Somerdale station.

The long familiar 'FRY' illuminated sign was replaced by 'Cadbury' in 1982, to the distress of local residents. This 1982 picture shows 'FRY SOMERDALE', which was still clearly visible on buildings on the north side until they were demolished in 1993.

The Fry train crossing the Willsbridge Road in 1962 with its load of chocolate. It ran twice daily, to and from the main GWR line.

'The Chocolate Line' leading from the main line through its cutting towards special sidings to the north-east of the factory.

The end of the line. The last Fry train ran in September 1978; the rails were lifted except under the road, and the cutting has since become overgrown.

The Roman well discovered in 1922 near a small Roman villa when Fry's No. 2 block was being constructed. The well still exists and is now listed.

In 1991 the levelling of a rugby pitch revealed remains of a Roman settlement and road. Much of this unfortunately was swept away before contractors realized its significance. Local archaeologists are still voluntarily rescuing artefacts from the dumped spoil for Cadbury's. Pottery seen here includes fine Samian ware from central Gaul, AD 125, mortaria rims and sherds of pots and bowls.

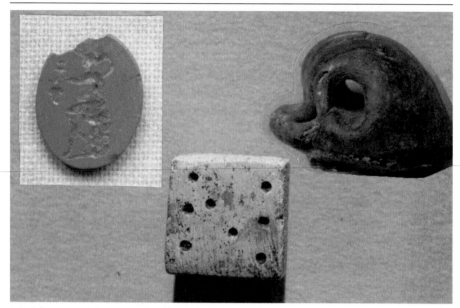

In addition to millions of pottery sherds dating from *c.* AD 80 to 400, the archaeologists recovered a ring bezel of carnelian engraved with a Bacchanalian figure (Bacchus was the god of wine, worshipped by humble folk, especially women, who worked themselves into an intoxicated mystical frenzy), a glass head of a dolphin, and an unusual die with two sides showing eight holes.

Other rescued artefacts include these bronze manicure implements: tweezers, cuticle removers and nail cleaners. Those with holes in the handle would have formed part of a set which hung from a ring.

Cutting the bypass through Memorial Park began in 1964. The line of the road is marked by fencing and the houses at the top of the hill are about to be demolished. Alterations to the River Chew are taking place in the foreground.

The new bridge over the Chew is under construction and roadworks progress. The old 'Abbot's Fishpond' has been destroyed, as have the houses on the hill. (S.R.)

The Park shortly before the demolition of the row of houses and realignment of the road.

Relics of Keynsham Abbey decorating the rockery of Abbotsford, one of the houses demolished off The Park. Many gardens contained carved stones dug up on the site of the abbey during house construction at the end of the nineteenth century. These were rescued by the archaeologists and stored by Fry's. The head of the figure (probably an abbot) was unfortunately stolen from the museum. We would welcome its reunion with its body.

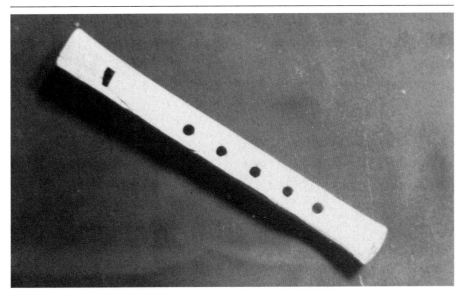

A thirteenth-century fipple flute, made from the bone of fallow deer, was excavated in the garden of Abbotsford and restored by the archaeologists.

Chandos House (centre) and the old Free School built in 1838, which were demolished for the bypass. Chandos House was for many years (*c.* 1769–1890) occupied by a succession of surgeons: Coke, Palmer, Palmer, Vaughan, Adams and Crisp. Capt. Frank Tennant lived here from 1919 until the end of the Second World War. On the left is the Pioneer Inn, formerly the White Horse (*c.* 1769–1859) but probably rebuilt. It has recently changed names several times: McGuiness, Boar's Head, Fontelles, and back to Pioneer.

Station Road bridge over the bypass, under construction. The old road had to be diverted while work was in progress.

A fine well revealed by machinery in the bypass close to the fence near The Park.

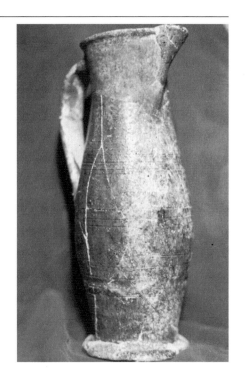

A thirteenth-century Saintonge (France) ware jug, 13 in. tall, which was found in a large culvert revealed by roadworks and restored by the voluntary archaeologists.

Head of a Green Man, a Romanesque sculpture recovered from rubble near the abbey's chapter house door. He has leaves in his hair, and probably also had foliage sprouting from his mouth. The Green Man was a pagan symbol representing the May King of May Day, who feigned death and then came back to life, thereby suggesting regeneration and fertility. In Christian imagery it became symbolic of Easter and the Resurrection.

Remains of Keynsham Abbey, now reburied, showing a slype (passageway) and spiral stairway leading off the East Cloister walk, on the east side of the bypass.

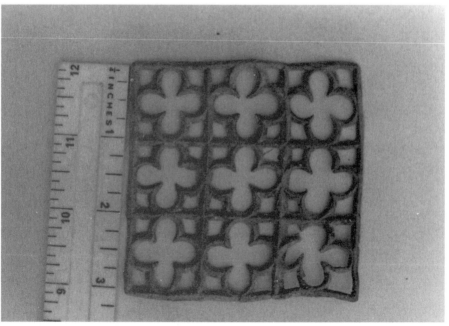

A ventilation panel of lead filigree, which was originally inserted in one of the abbey's windows. It was recovered from rubble in the bypass.

The Old Vicarage, rebuilt in the eighteenth century and extended in 1855. The building attached to the right of the main house was the original Free School built by Sir Thomas Bridges in 1705. This was incorporated into the vicarage when the new school was built in 1835. It was used as a soup kitchen, *c.* 1890.

Rear view of the Old Vicarage showing the unusual tall window inserted during the alterations of 1855.

Continuation of the right-hand side of the previous picture, showing part of the large garden and the rear of the coach house and Beech House.

The town houses built on the site of the Old Vicarage, Beech House, The Wingrove, Uplands House, etc, from 1973 to 1977. Cooper & Tanner occupied Beech House until it was demolished and Eddie Morgan ran his hairdressing business from the top floor of the coach house (approached by an external stair). Photographed in 1979.

Dowsing in 1970 failed to locate the two vicarage wells but developers of the site found two, one belonging to the Old Vicarage, the other near the coach house in 1972. Here, Michael Collins, a Mendip cave diver, is about to descend the vicarage well, assisted by archaeologists Barbara Lowe and Douglas Sprague. (S.R.)

The Old Vicarage well which was partially blocked with large stone rubble and was 30 ft deep.

Tombstones of our forebears attractively surround Keynsham Church in this 1930s' photograph. All these interesting family memorials were deliberately destroyed and used as rubble in 1957 and 1958, to save money on grass cutting. Some of the flat headstones were laid as paths, but wear and weather have now ruined the inscriptions.

The interior of Keynsham Church as it was in 1912. The locally made brass candelabra were donated by Ann Tillie in 1717 and 1721. Around the chancel arch are the words 'Thy Throne O God is for Ever and Ever'. The east window glass was donated in memory of the Stephens family after the previous window had fallen out in 1848. This was in turn replaced by modern glass in 1961.

The Keynsham bells were lowered in May 1987 and taken away to be renovated. The third bell, dated 1654, is here seen being lowered.

Four of the bells with their stocks await transport to the foundry.

The clappers of the bells carefully collected together in the church.

Aerial view of Keynsham in 1927, looking north. Compare sites in the north (Vicarage) and north-west (St John's Court) with the next two pictures.

Town houses cover the site of the Old Vicarage and land seen to the north of the church in the previous photo.

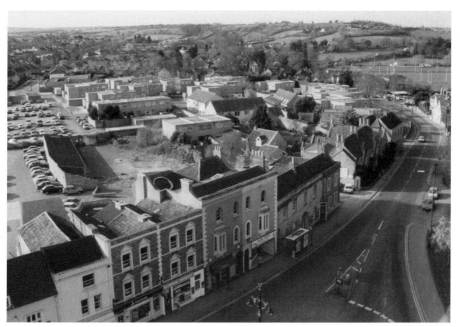

St John's Court and car parks cover the site north-west of the church, pictured opposite (bottom).

Bath Street (now Bristol Road) in 1907 showing Wingrove Hotel on the right. Notice the large lantern over the door. The whole rank as far as the cart was destroyed. On the left, the house between those with railings was also demolished. The Old Manor is turreted and Milward House, extreme left, is now rail-less.

Hawkeswell, now covered, was in the field beyond the Vicarage Green development. The well's water was once believed to cure eye complaints.

Bath Street, south side, with housing lining the hillside down Bristol Hill. All except the first were destroyed between 1969 and 1973, as were all those further down the hill, shown in the next photo.

Grass now replaces these homes and flat-roofed, two-storey blocks of flats, set back from the road, cover the site of their large gardens. See bottom p. 31.

Looking back up Bath Street towards the church at the same row of houses. (D.E.)

Bristol Road at its junction with St Ladoc. The cottages on the corner of St Ladoc, left, were demolished in the early 1960s, and replaced with a block of town houses. The row of three houses on the right still stands, but is empty. It was converted into two houses many years ago.

The trimobile, the Avon light delivery van, a two-seater with top speed of 20 mph. It was classed as a motor cycle, so fourteen-year-old A.E. Cannock was allowed to drive his aunt, Miss E. Cox, and her dog in 1911. The Avon Motor Manufacturing Co., Bath Road, produced the vehicle. The proprietor was George Henshaw.

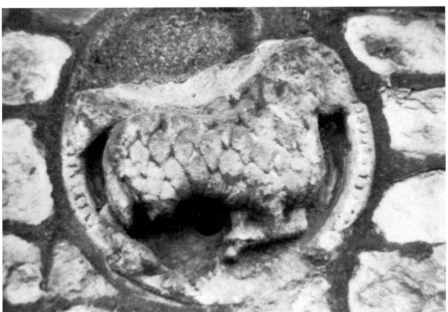

An embossed keystone, depicting the Agnus Dei, from the Romanesque refectory of Keynsham Abbey is now embedded in the front wall of the Crown Inn, Bristol Road. Three others, now internationally famous, were recovered from the bypass cutting.

Construction of the ring road north of Hick's Gate in 1993. Len Coggins, former LHS photograph archivist, is seen photographing a sprinter train passing the railway bridge under construction.

Another view of the construction in 1993 of the river and rail bridges near Hick's Gate.

Electricity showrooms, 1960, formerly the Railway Tavern which closed in 1956. The latter had been rebuilt on part of the site of the Black Horse after the opening of the railway. Harper's fruit and vegetable shop is on the right.

The same scene in 1991. The lane on the left once gave access to Parfitt and Webber's electricity works situated on the site of the present Parish Hall.

The two cottages (left), demolished in the 1960s, were replaced by featureless flat-roofed shop units, seen to the right in the last photo. One is now Cornerstones; the other is vacant (formerly Kiosks). Pictured in the centre is Pearsall's, formerly Parker's toys, and Elizabethan Pine, formerly Beer's, then Milton's and Hayman's.

Woolworths, built on the site of three cottages in 1955, closed in January 1989; its loss is greatly lamented.

TSB rebuilt on the Woolworths site and moved in during the autumn of 1989.

General view, 1967, with the Royal Oak in the centre. This was renamed The London in 1974 after the old Temple Street inn was demolished and its landlord, Bert Simpkins, moved to the Royal Oak.

The Forresters Arms, left, was kept by postman Dick Harris from 1910 to 1935, and by Harriet House before that. Bristol Co-operative Society (centre) moved from the other side of the road (no. 10) to this site, which was formerly Herbert's grocery shop. Christopher James Kohler moved before 1902 from the site lately occupied by Halfords and was still here at Chard House in 1939. (D.E.)

Here, part of the premises sells shoes, later electrical goods. In 1987, Clive, the hairdressers, and Maggs, electrical goods, occupied the site.

The Midland Bank here occupies Longton House. A ladies' school was held in this house before the turn of the century; it later became a mixed school run by Miss Fry and cost 9*d* a week.

Children from the school run by Edith Shellard (1902) and Ellen Mee until 1910.

Miss Rachel Ann Spiller was running Keynsham post office by 1875. She married Charles Harvey, who owned the house. Notice the parish pump on the extreme left.

A.E. Mills bought the building in 1925 and Mills & Mills, the chemists, became well known. Indigo, Shaggers and Thornton's recently occupied the site.

Now a sports shop, this house was occupied by Mr Hickling, manager of Valley Water Mills Colour Co. The entrance to Back Lane and the old coach house (now demolished) are seen on the left. Before the Baptist Chapel was built, Back Lane ran from Pump Court, behind Mills & Mills and behind Lloyds Bank.

Percy Baker's tailor's shop was next door, no. 43. Later, he moved across the road near the Fear Institute. He was the last chairman of Keynsham Urban District Council (KUDC) in 1974.

R. Hall & Sons' toy shop and newsagent at no. 43, later Abbey Park Pharmacy. The demolition area was where Bailey and Maddicks' motor engineering business stood. Cars drove through the building into workshops on the other side of Back Lane.

This was the site of Keynsham's first picture house, 1904–18, which was rebuilt as Walter Beak's engineering business and later named St Keyna Motor Works. This was demolished in 1960.

Halfords, rebuilt on the site of the Motor Works, has recently closed. Seafoods, left, and seen in the two previous photos, is one of the oldest properties in the row.

R. Hall & Sons and these cottages, also seen to the right of the picture opposite (bottom), were then demolished. Currently, Menzies, the newsagents, a betting shop and the Cook Shop occupy the site.

Strudwick's ironmonger's occupied this disused Wesleyan Chapel from 1936 until 1983. The site for the chapel was bought for £45 in 1803 from William Malpass. The congregation vacated it in 1887 when the new Victoria Methodist Church opened over the road. The Halifax Building Society bought it in 1983.

This has been a tailor/outfitter's since 1896 when Newport Brothers opened their shop. A sign outside the shop read: 'Bristol 4½ miles, Newport's 4½ yards'. Edward Joll, father of the present owner, bought the shop in the early 1930s. Notice the original shop front of 1896.

A well discovered during renovation of the Oxfam shop in 1987. The south wall of Joll's shop (top of picture) was built over the well.

No. 59 received a direct hit in 1940. The occupant was Mrs B.M. Carter who ran the well-known china shop (see bottom of p. 54). She had built the tiny shop between nos 59 and 61, now incorporated into New Look, but previously Halliday's, then Jolyon's, the hairdressers.

To the left, John Lee Carter & Sons, undertakers and carpenters, ran their business here from 1894 until *c.* 1939. The house was demolished in the 1960s and Fads now occupies the rebuilt shop unit. The central house was formerly Heal's ironmongery, then Somerdale bakery, then Tompkins' and Springers'.

The fire station decked out for George V's Silver Jubilee in 1935. Formerly a coach house, it was the fire station from 1928 until it was demolished in 1965. It is seen to the right of Tompkins' in the 1959 picture above. Currys presently occupies the redeveloped site.

Ernie Wiltshire's paint, wallpaper and hardware shop, left, formerly Shepherd's Boot Warehouse and Rose's Bootmakers, demolished in 1965. Currys and Bradford & Bingley occupy the site. Centre is Paula Thomson's draper's shop, formerly Brownsey, the butcher, and later, Ogborn's.

Rawling's cycle shop, right, now houses an optician and turf accountant. In the centre is Mervyn Holmes, later Nix's Garden and Pet Shop, with Ogborn's Newsagents (closed 1991 to the left.

A superb panoramic view showing the Lamb & Lark Hotel crowning the hilltop. Documented since 1745 but older, it was used for important meetings, for the Feoffees who administered Keynsham's charities, for balls, as an Inland Revenue office and as a Magistrates' Court. Its demolition early one Sunday morning in 1971, to be replaced with what is now Somerfield and Ronto's, was criminal vandalism. (S.R.)

On the left of the above picture were the offices of F.J. Ollis & Sons' Haulage and Removal business and a tiny hardware shop. The latter was presided over by Mr Ollis who lived in the house. It is now a pizzeria.

Billhead of the Lamb & Lark Hotel in 1875 when
Betsy Skuse was licensee.

Tangent Tool Engineering Co. employees gathering outside the Lamb & Lark for an
outing in the early 1920s. This company, of Long Reach, Bath Road, built the
Keynsham Lawn Mower, and was the successor to the Avon Motor Manufacturing
Company.

Keynsham & District Horticultural Society advertising their annual show on the yard gates of the Lamb & Lark early this century.

In 1956 the gates had long gone and the car god is in the ascendant. Vans hide the entrance to the famous Palm Court and the lane behind the motor bike gives access to another car park.

Thomas Stroud ran his greengrocery business here after the First World War, changing to confectionery in the late 1920s. In 1985 Eric and Margaret Church celebrated fifty years of a family business started by his father. The shop now incorporates Arthur's small Fruit Market.

A modern view of High Street showing the two older properties right of Church's, and the stark modern development beyond.

Smart's is now part of Buss's greengrocery, Bollom is now Tripp's photographers, and Luton's bakery has become Tastebuds. Gas Service, Fray's, Carter's and every building as far as the present Revelations were destroyed and a new row built, set back from the road.

Mrs Carter boasted of always keeping 101 tea services in her lovely china shop and it still evokes nostalgia.

Buss's and Tripp's modern shop fronts belie the age of their buildings. Rebuilding at the rear of these sixteenth-century shops in 1988 revealed carved abbey masonry forming part of a bread oven.

During the same rebuilding this beautiful section of a medieval wooden screen was found re-used as a window lintel.

Hodges, now Dunn's, is on the site of the former Gas Service house (see top of p. 54). An outhouse to the rear of the old house in 1849, occupied by William Cantle, was used by Wesleyan Methodists who broke away from the old Chapel.

Tregare House, centre, was the home of the well-respected Dr Charles Harrison and his son 'Dr Claud'. It is seen here in 1959 under demolition. The present post office occupies the site. To the extreme left is the Co-op Drapery store, formerly Parsons'. To the right of Brook's was Hodder's the chemist.

The house, left, was John Loxton's Drapers from some time before 1889 to 1927 when T.C. Parsons took over.

Dr Harrison's house showing the low-roofed surgery to its left. The hardware department of the Co-op is seen on the extreme left. The destruction of all these buildings, coupled with that of the Lamb & Lark, completely robbed Keynsham High Street of all its character – and to what advantage?

R.D. Hickling's much loved ironmonger's shop. He took over the shop when his friend, John Henry Down, who started the business, died suddenly in 1906. Notice the adverts: Cranes fireworks, Mobiloils, Starex roofing, Siemens cement, Abol insecticide.

Whitings furniture shop next to Victoria Methodist Church was part of the Bristol firm which employed up to 570 people making cinema seats for worldwide distribution. The shop moved here from over the road betwen 1973 and 1974. The site is now occupied by Revelations and The Wine Rack.

Reynolds Brothers corner shop in 1959. Next to it, right, was Stafford's shoe shop, and Morgan's hair stylist.

Charlton Road in 1957, showing the pleasant buildings demolished to make way for the featureless block in which the Chew Valley Restaurant is housed. (D.E.)

Reynolds' corner under demolition. Before 1910, the house, right, was the Employment Exchange, run by Fred Dorey. He was registrar for births and deaths when his father was master of the workhouse.

Conflagration! In August 1978 fire swept through the furnishing shop of Organ & Davis. This block was built on the site of Reynolds. After the fire it was renovated and is now the Midland Bank.

Miss Grace Fairclough established her milliner's shop here before the First World War. The house was demolished in 1937 to build the Fear Institute.

John Nelson Fear, manager of the gas works and a prominent Methodist, left a legacy with which to build the Institute.

The house and shop which now comprise the National Westminster Bank, formerly the National Provincial and Bristol Old Bank. Bristol Co-op stores later absorbed William Pearce's bakery.

Bristol Co-operative Society Grocery Stores in 1970. It later became Co-op Freezer Centre and now has been refronted as CRS Funeral Services. On the right is the Conservative Club which moved here from two converted cottages off Bristol Road, c. 1910.

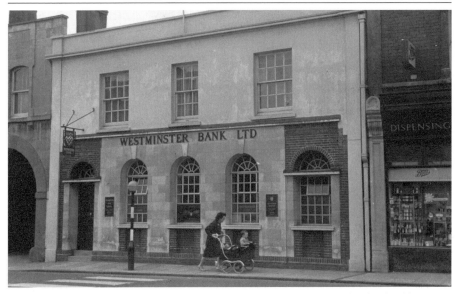

Westminster Bank before its merger with the National Provincial. The building was adapted to become the Kimberly Wine Bar, then Porter & Fodder in 1987, and now, appropriately, The Old Bank. Boots is seen to the right.

In 1994 Starzec's Shoeshop celebrated twenty-five years in the old Boots shop (unavoidable pun!), formerly Robertson's. John Down had started his ironmongery business here by 1889, later moving to Hickling's site. Pearce's became Church Bakery, with long queues during the bread strike, and is now a solicitor's.

West End House, reputed site of the fifteenth-century St John's Hospice. Mitchell's is now Ballaarat Wines and, right, International Stores became Room Robes and now, Roger Appleton. Before the First World War, George E. Chappell moved his grocery business here. West End Radio's bow window has vanished. Bristol Co-op was here, c. 1910, and latterly Courtnay's.

Exons Dairy was taken over by Unigate, which moved out some ten years ago. This post office closed when the new one was built in the High Street.

Ancient Back Lane seen from Lloyds Bank end, before its obliteration in 1989. Local voluntary archaeologists were allowed a bare twenty-eight days in July 1988 to hand-excavate behind the door on the left.

Archaeologists and LHS members at work: Mike Hutchings, Marianne Rice, Lorna Wood, Ann Starr, Diana McCall, Margaret Whitehead and Barbara Lowe.

After clearing nettles, glass, rubbish, tins, etc., without machinery, and shifting tons of earth, on the very last day we were allowed on the site the above foundation walls were located. There was no time to excavate deeper. Subsequent documentary evidence proved that three sixteenth-century cottages on the site were demolished, c. 1850.

The old footbridge, erected in 1838, from the former Wesleyan Chapel across Back Lane to their Sunday school.

The Bath Hill end of Back Lane in 1988, looking north.

A record of the period of two and a half years when the ancient right of way was closed to the public by Taylor Woodrow. Back Lane had already been obliterated and replaced with a road. High Street traders were deprived of access to the rear of their businesses.

The Old Liberal Club, left, which became Keynsham's first public library, later Pagoda Chinese Restaurant (1966), then a carpet shop and Bizzy-Bee printer, before being demolished. The Old Court House, centre, was the site of the seventeenth-century Manorial Court and used as a police station until 1858.

Save Me! We tried but failed. Yet another Keynsham listed building was allowed to fall down (1979) so that redevelopment of Back Lane could proceed.

The Victorian police station, built in 1858 and extended by 1883 for use as a Magistrates' Court. It was demolished in 1972 to provide a car park for the new police station and courts. The latter were closed in 1990, thus ending Keynsham's 800-year-old right to hold court.

Wellsway/Bath Road junction, c. 1900. Off to the extreme left was the site of the Manor & Hundred's Pound. To the left of the Talbot (with carts and wagons), lawns replace the tall house.

Keynsham cattle market, *c.* 1950. Cooper & Tanner (auctioneers) leased this site (seen to right of the inn in last photo) from George's Brewery from 1923 to 1975. The site is now covered by HomeAvon blocks of flats.

Prospective buyers cluster around the covered part of the market (1974) where furniture was often auctioned.

Who will buy my fine turkey? See the feathers flying as Christmas turkeys are auctioned, c. 1935.

The cattle pens at Keynsham's very busy market in the 1950s. Lionel Smart, Joe Taylor, John Withers and Fred Mathews are present. (D.E.)

The end of a busy day. To the right of the animal-weighing machine stands Gordon Dunn.

The grassy slope in the distance, right, was the site of Fairfield Terrace (nineteen cottages) and Woodbine Steps (eleven cottages), demolished in 1974. In 1879 C. Harvey built two homes in an orchard in Poggam's Lane but, encountering difficulties, he built the rest on a more level ledge facing the river.

Flander's House in 1951. This fine eighteenth-century house stood to the extreme left of the last picture on the other side of the river. James Racker held the title deeds, 1767–99, but the name was reputedly given by a predecessor who probably came from Holland. After the road was raised in 1839, the house was left below its level.

The garden and rear view of Flander's House which was demolished c. 1964. The whole site became yet another car park in 1993.

Cheapside. Gilbert's shoe shop, formerly the Oxford café, was a butcher's shop with a slaughterhouse behind in 1841. By 1875, Edward Down, great-grandfather of Margaret Whitehead, was carrying on the butcher's trade, followed by Alice Fisher until the 1930s. Subsequently E. Chinnock opened a café before the Second World War.

Cheapside being demolished in 1962. The row once contained bakers (Parsons, Beale, Herbert), boot makers (White, Cains), the first Co-op, a sweep (Sweet), haulier (Crease), the Rising Sun, and decorators (Bailey – also undertakers).

The lower end of Cheapside, looking up the hill. One of these housed a small private school early this century, costing 6*d* (2½p) a week.

Keynsham Civic Centre which was opened in October 1965, by Major Sir Egbert Cadbury. The town hall now houses the planning department of Wansdyke District

The lane on the left, beyond the slaughterhouse, gave access to the area behind Cheapside. Once known as the Barton, it was thought to have been a market place. Beyond Sherer's and Cavendish's was the Wheatsheaf (1894–1902), later Hines (chimney sweep).

Cottages await demolition for the erection of new shops and fire station.

The Drumway to Prospect Place cottages. This entrance is left of the bus stop in the previous photo.

Old cobbled path of the Drumway with an ancient covered drain down the centre (for stormwater). The path ran down to the right to join a path to the Labbott.

The east side of Temple Street was demolished, thereby destroying a close-knit community.

The surnames Bees, Veale, Williams, Cantle, Crew, Townsend, Carpenter, Newman, Ollis, Robbins, Fray, Ford, Cox, Rayson, Sweet and Godfrey were well known in Temple Street.

Mrs Townsend's small shop on the corner of the path to the Labbott with her son George at the door, early 1900s. At this time sugar was 2*d* a pound and eighteen eggs cost 1*s*. See also top p. 89.

Leaning on the gate! After walkies in the Labbott? Miss Wellington had a fish and chip shop nearby.

View from the Labbott of the front of the four Prospect Place cottages and three others in the Labbott prior to their demolition.

Phase two of the Temple Street scheme just before these cottages disappeared in 1964.

Possibly the coffin of Job Sweet, chimney sweep, who died in 1913. He lived here at no. 63.

The London Inn, no. 71, was left isolated between 1967 and 1973 when pleas for its conservation failed.

Ten cottages between the London and Ship Inns were demolished in 1967.

The seventeenth-century Ship is the only listed building to survive along this side of Temple Street.

A row of pleasant cottages between the Ship and the Zion Primitive Methodist Church. All were demolished in 1966.

The Zion Primitive Methodist Church which was opened in 1861, having been built by members who started their congregation in Joseph Cantle's cottage next door, right.

Cottages between Zion and The Pines, Dapps Hill. These were demolished in the early 1960s.

Coach house cottage belonging to The Pines, a large house with superb gardens which swept down to the river.

Dapps Hill showing the gateposts, all that is left of The Pines and coach house. This is now a conservation area.

Dapps (or Dabbs) Hill Farm on the high embankment opposite The Pines site. It, too, was demolished but the small dairy, left, has been well restored as a house.

Dapps Hill Farm from the rear, showing various later additions.

Old London Inn, left, looking towards Cranmore House, centre. At least one cottage in the row dated to the sixteenth century but all were demolished in 1970. The corner of Carpenter's Lane on the extreme right is where Granny Townsend had her shop specializing in her bread-and-butter puddings. William Veale's butcher's shop was at the end.

Tamsin Court replaced these old cottages.

All gone for ever. This row was demolished during the late 1960s and early 1970s.

Four cottages between Causes Lane, left, and Bethesda Methodist Church, were demolished to make Carpenter's Lane.

The Trout Inn was rebuilt in 1800. The shop, left, was Horace Veale's grocery (*c.* 1902–32), and is now Dr Barnardo's.

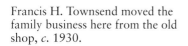

Francis H. Townsend moved the family business here from the old shop, *c.* 1930.

The same building with a modernized front. Tina's closed in 1988 and the building was recently renovated as a Chinese take-away.

A carved stone head (dating back to the twelfth or thirteenth century) from Keynsham Abbey. It was built into a garden wall at the rear of Tina's, but it disappeared when Tina's closed.

The *Keynsham Chronicle* office. Its first office was on the ground floor of the old library. The last edition was in November 1992 and Keynsham is now starved of a local newspaper.

The row of shops from the Trout to Diana Fox Interiors is listed and nos 20–32 are being sympathetically renovated (1993/4).

Looking north, *c.* 1900, showing Cridlands Stores on the corner of Rock Road. For a few years after Queen Victoria's Diamond Jubilee in 1897, the section between Rock Road and Carpenter's Lane was called Victoria Street.

The Three Horse Shoes Inn and Willoughby's, the grocer's, seen from Grimes (which replaced Cridlands) at the corner of Rock Road. Willoughby's was the last Keynsham grocer to serve across the counter.

Charles Richard Willoughby with his staff, standing outside the shop he opened in c. 1890 with Mr Tame. Right up until 1968, when the business closed, a member of staff would come to the customer's house to take the weekly order and then deliver it later in the week.

SECTION TWO
Water Power

Prince Philip visiting Dapps Hill on 15 July 1968 after Keynsham had been declared a disaster area following the floods on 10 July. In a helicopter of the Queen's Flight, he landed at Fry's, with Somerdale Fire Brigade in attendance.

Stanton Drew bridge on 11 July, and efforts to repair the flood damage of the previous night. There was a rainfall of 7½ in. in the Bath area and a wall of water swept down the River Chew at about 1 a.m., damaging or destroying every bridge in its path.

Pensford showing the Bailey bridge which was erected by Royal Engineers across the severely ruptured roadbridge.

Publow Bridge in August 1968. Less severely damaged, it was possible to brace the foundations with concrete and resurface it.

The Chewton–Keynsham road at 7 a.m. on 11 July 1968. The parapets suffered badly and walls were destroyed. Boys from King Edward's School, Bath, spent the day assisting those who had suffered damage.

Croxbottom. The damaged Dapps Hill Bridge on 11 July. Volunteers gathered to help the residents with their flooded homes.

Memorial Park seen from the bypass bridge on 11 July. The remains of Downe Mill can be seen in the centre and part of the bandstand on the extreme left.

The wreckage of the children's playground off Avon Mill Lane, later in the day of 11 July, when the water had receded a little.

Town Bridge (Downe Bridge) at the bottom of Bath Hill, after a hole appeared in it, rendering it unsafe. Pedestrians and traffic had to use the bypass to travel from one side of Keynsham to the other.

The Fox and Hounds Inn, pictured in 1906, was bought by the council and demolished in 1963. This stood to the right of the terrace of houses and shops seen in the picture below. [M.T.]

This early twentieth-century row, just east of the Town Bridge, took the full force of the floodwater. The buildings were all demolished because the road had to be raised by 3 ft to line up with the proposed new bridge.

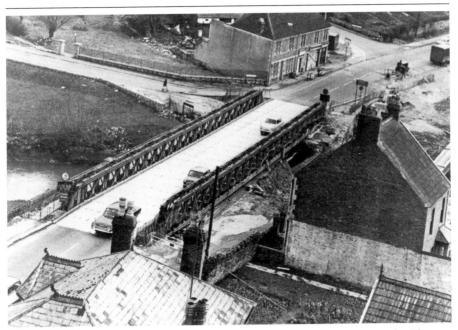

Bailey bridge erected by 60 Field Squadron 36 Engineering Regiment over the Chew at the bottom of Bath Hill. (S.R.)

Consternation at the Willsbridge Road end of Avon Mill Lane. Cables can be seen floating in the swollen river.

Avon Mill Lane reached an abrupt end after Pollard's Bridge was swept away. Notice the damaged wall of the Avon Mill buildings.

The thirteenth-century County Bridge was beyond repair. Here a Bailey bridge allows access from Somerset to Gloucestershire. The large stone fondly called The Abbot's Chair was swept on to Fry's meadow but was later rescued and is now in council care.

Side view of the Bailey bridge showing clearance work on the remains of the ancient bridge. (S.R.)

Part of the new County Bridge being constructed on a totally different alignment from the ancient one. (S.R.)

The old steel mill building (recently renovated) in Steel Mills Lane. In 1749 Christopher Shallard occupied the mill but by 1814 the steel works were for sale. In 1834 Philip Jones occupied it and later, Robert Ruddle.

The garden in which two steel furnaces once stood. In 1815 the steelworks complex consisted of a dwelling-house, gardens, stable, orchard, two steel furnaces with a smith's shop, warehouse, charcoal house and barton, and a mill house with newly erected hammer mill and 8 hp steam engine.

Albert Mill, *c.* 1937, looking south. Notice the pile of dyewood in the yard. The last commercial load was processed in 1964. It had been a woollen mill in the 1770s, later spinning cotton and flax. Rebuilt as a corn mill by 1836, it was then adapted for crushing lime and ochre.

The same view in the late 1960s, showing neglect and dilapidation. It was named Albert Mill after the fire of 1873 and used to process logwood. In 1951 it produced Glauber Salts and ammonium chloride.

Mr Septimus Price, *c.* 1951, drawing off acetic acid into a large carboy. He was one of a large family of Welsh extraction who had lived in Steel Mills for several generations and worked at Albert Mill.

Albert Mill weir as it was in 1951, before alterations following the 1968 flood.

This idyllic view of the south and east sides of Albert Mill was taken *c.* 1960. Left, in front of the main building was the Glauber Salts house.

A 1994 view of the same side of the mill. Extensive redevelopment of the site has taken place but the character of the main building has been retained.

Downe Mill which was demolished *c.* 1948 when KUDC bought the former Abbey Precinct to make a public park. The weir and millwheel remain.

Avon Mill in 1928, shortly before the cone tower (which housed annealing ovens) was demolished. The works closed in 1927 and most buildings were demolished in the 1930s.

SECTION THREE
Duty and Leisure

Keynsham Town Silver Band was formed 1922–4. In 1924 the instruments cost £725, paid for by Captain Wills of Corston. Albert Townsend was bandmaster in the 1920s.

Keynsham Lacrosse Team 1913–14, having won the west of England W.D. and H.O. Wills' Challenge Flag. The Revd Noel Cooke is seated, front left, and Sidney N. Fairclough (father of Mary) is in the back row, second from right.

The lacrosse team of 1921–2, after winning the Wills' Junior Challenge Flag. Left to right, front row: H. Neat, -?-, J. Down, L. Bowden, K. Gibbons, E. Blake, F. Martin, E. Loxton, S. Parsons, M. Gibbons. Middle row: -?-, -?-, -?-, Rex Harris, J. Stickler, C.P. Gibbons, H. Rogers, N. Batty, W.R. Gibbons, H. Smith, C. Stokes, -?-. Top row: -?-, E. Stokes (above), M. Scears, L. Neat, -?- (above), Revd Southall.

The Mikado or *Town of Titipu* by Keynsham & District Amateur Operatic Society, held at the Drill Hall, January 1920. In the programme 'Ladies are requested to remove their hats'.

The cast list from the programme for the above show. Notice the advertisements. The programme cost 2d.

The Rose of Persia by the same society, held at the Drill Hall in April 1929. Irene Down (née Taylor), mother of Margaret Whitehead, is seen lying front right.

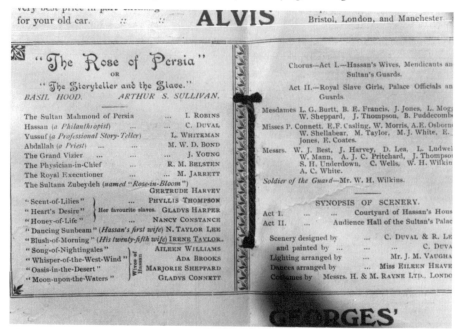

" The Rose of Persia "
OR
" The Storyteller and the Slave."
BASIL HOOD.   *ARTHUR S. SULLIVAN.*

The Sultan Mahmoud of Persia	...	I. ROBINS
Hassan (*a Philanthropist*)	...	C. DUVAL
Yussuf (*a Professional Story-Teller*)		L. WHITMAN
Abdallah (*a Priest*)	...	M. W. D. BOND
The Grand Vizier	...	...	J. YOUNG
The Physician-in-Chief	...	R. M. BELSTEN
The Royal Executioner	...	M. JARRETT
The Sultana Zubeydeh (*named "Rose-in-Bloom"*)		GERTRUDE HARVEY

"Scent-of-Lilies"   ... PHYLLIS THOMPSON
"Heart's Desire" } Her favourite slaves. GLADYS HARPER
"Honey-of-Life"   ... NANCY CONSTANCE
"Dancing Sunbeam" (*Hassan's first wife*) N. TAYLOR LEE
"Blush-of-Morning" (*His twenty-fifth wife*) IRENE TAYLOR
"Song-of-Nightingales"   AILEEN WILLIAMS
"Whisper-of-the-West-Wind" } ADA BROOKS
"Oasis-in-the-Desert" } MARJORIE SHEPPARD
"Moon-upon-the-Waters"   GLADYS CONNETT

Chorus—Act I.—Hassan's Wives, Mendicants an
Sultan's Guards.

Act II.—Royal Slave Girls, Palace Officials an
Guards.

Mesdames L. G. Burtt, B. E. Francis, J. Jones, L. Mog
W. Sheppard, J. Thompson, B. Puddecomb
Misses P. Connett, E.F. Casling, W. Morris, A.E. Osborn
W. Shellabear, M. Taylor, M.J. White, E.
Jones, E. Coates.
Messrs. W. J. Best, J. Harvey, D. Lea, L. Ludwel
W. Mann, A. J. C. Pritchard, J. Thompso
S. H. Underdown, C. Wells, W. H. Wilkin
A. C. White.

Soldier of the Guard—Mr. W. H. Wilkins.

SYNOPSIS OF SCENERY.

Act I.	...	...	Courtyard of Hassan's Hous
Act II.	...	Audience Hall of the Sultan's Palac

Scenery designed by   ... C. DUVAL & R. LE
and painted by ...   . C. DUVA
Lighting arranged by   ... Mr. J. M. VAUGHA
Dances arranged by   ... Miss EILEEN HEAVE
Costumes by Messrs. H. & M. RAYNE LTD., LONDO

The cast list from the programme for the show – but the cost has risen to 6*d*.

Bath Hill School, c. 1900.

Block by Bristol Photo Engraving Co. Ltd., Broad Street, Bristol.

Keynsbam 41st Annual Flower Show

THE SHOW OF THE WEST

August Bank Holiday, Monday & Tuesday, 5th & 6th.

Number of Entries for 1928 - **1,085**

Attendance - - - - **15,151**

Prize Money Offered - - **£350**

Special attention is called to the extension of the area for Cottagers and Amateurs >>>

Latest Music for Dancing, and Novelties
will be supplied by

Badman's Marconiphone Amplifiers both days.

The most Efficient and Up-to-date *Come and Listen to the Best Music.*

Dance and Enjoy yourselves!!!

Advertisement for the 1929 Keynsham Flower Show. This was a great annual event and everyone competed for the generous prizes offered.

111

Keynsham Flower Show in 1930. Frederick Vowles (centre) was chairman of the show. He was Rex Harris's father-in-law and lived at Abbey Meade, The Park.

The practice nets at Somerdale, *c.* 1930. Keynsham folk have always taken their sport seriously.

Zenana handkerchief stall. Mrs Clara Fairclough (grandmother of Mary, local artist, author and historian) is in charge.

KEYNSHAM PARISH CHURCH.

The *Heating Apparatus* in our Church is worn and old,
And unless we get a new one we shall all be very cold.
It will cost a lot of money, and be very dear to buy,
Therefore, to raise the needful funds we all of us must try.
A SALE OF WORK is to be held, this coming Autumn time,
And the ladies all are working with energy sublime ;
I'm going to have a little Stall, nice HANDKERCHIEFS to sell,
And if you will but send me some, 'twill please me very well.
All kinds will be acceptable—quite large or very small,
For ladies or for gentlemen—I'm sure to sell them all.
So please you, of your charity, send me a little gift,
To help this worthy cause along—*and let your help be swift.*

(Mrs.) C. FAIRCLOUGH.

"OCKHAM,"
    KEYNSHAM.

An appealing rhyme for replacing the church heating apparatus.

Zenana handkerchief stall, 1936.

SALE OF WORK
MAY 27th. 28th.
— 1936 —

HANDKERCHIEF STALL

Once more comes the appeal
For our Schools, upon Bath Hill.
They need repair, and we all feel
We must help to pay the bill.

It's HANDKERCHIEFS *we* are asking for,
Of every kind and hue.
If you will send us one or more
We shall have quite a few.

To be without a HANDKERCHIEF
Is really quite distressing,
So if you will only send us one
'Twill surely prove a blessing.

Gifts to be sent to :

(Miss) D. FAIRCLOUGH,
12, PRIORY ROAD,
KEYNSHAM.

Miss D. Fairclough's rhyming appeal for repairs to Bath Hill School.

Keynsham's first picture house, *c.* 1914, in the High Street. It was here from 1904 to 1918, then, in 1936, the present cinema was built in Charlton Road.

Keynsham Town Band playing a fanfare at the opening of the cinema in 1936. The musicians included Joe James and members of the Harvey family.

Christabel Cooksley's Infant School, The Park, 1938. Left to right: F.B.O. Harris, Dick Yeoman, Roger ?, -?-, B.R.O. Harris, Alan Russett, John Stokes, Dick Stokes.

The same school, including the girls. Back row, left to right: Barry Harris, Dick Stokes, John Stokes, -?-. Middle row: Roger ?, Mary Stokes, Meg Gibbons, Audrey Gibbons, Alan Russett. Front row: Dick Yeoman, Priscilla Wilson, Brian Harris.

Keynsham Fire Service during the Second World War.

INSTRUCTIONS TO FIRE WATCHERS.

EQUIPMENT TO BE CARRIED BY EVERY FIRE WATCHER

ONE belt to go round waist with hooks (10) to support six full sandbags and four buckets of water.

ONE axe stuck in belt.

ONE stirrup pump to be carried over left shoulder.

ONE whistle to be carried in mouth - spare pea for same lodged in right ear.

ONE extending ladder to be carried over right shoulder.

ONE long handled shovel to be carried under left arm.

ONE crow bar to be tucked under right arm.

ONE dustbin lid to be carried in left hand.

TWO wet blankets to be carried on head.

ONE tin hat with turn up brim to carry spare water.

Spare sand to be carried in all pockets.

ONE box matches to light all incendiaries which fail to ignite.

ONE roll toilet paper to be slung on back, rip cord at "alert" over left ear, for immediate action and use.

Instructions issued to fire watchers.

Womens' Voluntary Service Salvage Drive during the Second World War.

Keynsham 2nd Platoon Home Guard, November 1944. Left to right, back row: L/C Thackway, Fox, White, Brearley, -?-. Middle row: -?-, Stabbins Jr, Whittuck, Turville, Stabbins Snr, Ryan, Buttle, Wiggins, Rose, Jenkins, Vowles. Front row: Cpl. Camsas, Cpl. Whittuck, Cpl. Owens, Lt. Membry, Capt. Meyer, Lt. Cormick, 1st Lt. Smailes, Sgt. Harris, Cpl. Taylor.

Keynsham Secondary Modern School football team 1948–9 included L. Miles, John Russell, D. Price and R. Trencham.

A map illustrating every facet of the history of Keynsham, drawn by Mary Fairclough for the Children's Library in the old Bath Hill premises. Centre top shows the abbey arms of six reversed clarions, and centre bottom, its thirteenth-century seal. People, events, farms, industries, transport, battles and wildlife are all exquisitely drawn.

The 1951 exhibition held in the Fear Institute showed the rich variety of Keynsham skills and interests. This corner display shows miniatures, bookbinding, old coins, model cabinets and Queen Victoria's stockings! Miss Shellabear stands right, front.

Queen's Road Coronation Party of 1953 with many children in fancy dress. Were you there?

The centre of Keynsham on the occasion of Queen Elizabeth's Silver Jubilee in 1977.

Pictured are Keynsham Urban District Councillors Baker, Ellis, Randall, Hayne, James, Prestridge, Miles, Sanders and Ashton. (S.R.)

Farewell to Somerset exhibition, 1974, organized by members of Keynsham & Saltford Local History Society in the Parish Hall. The exhibition included prehistoric, Roman and medieval artefacts, church plate, musical instruments, documents, crafts, costumes and brassware. In addition, Vitamealo and other industries, the fire brigade, bell ringers, clock makers and sports were all represented.

The brass industry display. The Fray bowl on the left and other vessels made locally have been donated to the above society for posterity.

Keynsham Carnival, 1974, and one the amusing floats.

Fry's grounds, the starting place for all Keynsham Carnivals. This scene in 1974 shows crowds gathering around the stalls.

These purple and white clad majorettes, with a 'D' on their attractive tall hats, formed a colourful and musical part of the 1974 carnival procession past the Town Hall.

Gentlemen drummers in navy and white march along the High Street as part of the same procession.

Teams from Keynsham and Saltford competing in the water carnival on Bathampton Canal in 1984.

Pageant float celebrating Fry's anniversary; the costumes depict the change in fashion of women's clothing over the previous 250 years.

'Make a Mosaic' day at Keynsham Library in August 1987. This was a two-hour practical session for children organized jointly by the librarian Linda Horne and trustees of the Keynsham & North Wansdyke Heritage Trust, assisted by young people from Avon County Council Environment Scheme.

Another Library Day held in 1989, showing the younger children waiting to begin their projects.

Stagecoach, driven by Mr Hoddinott, *c.* 1900. The coach was kept at the Ship Inn, Temple Street.

Historic re-run of the Royal Mail coach, August 1984, as it passed St Dunstan's Church, Keynsham. The coach was no. 200 VR.

Acknowledgements

Most of these photographs are from the archives of Keynsham & Saltford Local History Society, supplemented by those of the authors. We are deeply grateful to all those people who, over the years, have donated their photographs to the society or allowed us to copy them. Unfortunately, we do not now know all their names, so please forgive any omissions in the list below.

Mary Fairclough laid down the foundation of the collection and gradually added to it. Her excellent work was ably continued by Len Coggins who never let a Keynsham event pass unrecorded. Mr Bryan, former KUDC surveyor, kindly donated invaluable photographic records of the High Street and Temple Street before their wholesale destruction in the late 1950s and 1960s. In addition, we acknowledge with thanks photographs supplied by:

Miss Carpenter • Mrs J. Carter • Mrs B. Dunford • Mrs M. Dunn
Miss E. Fox • Miss M. Hamlyn • Miss M. Hickling • Miss J. Knight
Miss M. Lanning • A. Brown • E. Cannock • B. Cottle • M. Fisher
J. Gibbons • S. Grylls-Wilson • B. Harris • T. Joll • R.D. Lanning
P.F. Lowe • P.A. Lowe E.J. Mason • 'REM' • B. Moon
R. Scott • K. Thomas • R.T. Townsend • F. Willoughby

We are also most grateful to professional photographers Stuart Reeve (S.R.), David Elliott (D.E.) and M. Tozer (M.T.), for their cooperation and generosity in allowing us to reproduce their photographs.

Connie Smith's archival work, and reminiscences of local residents, have greatly helped the provision of interesting captions for the pictures. More detailed information is provided in the following: Joan Day's *Guide to Industrial Heritage of Avon*, 1987; *Keynsham Abbey Excavations 1961–85*, in Proc. Somerset Arch. & Nat. Hist. Soc. vol. 131, 1987; *The History of Keynsham 1538–1945*, 1994; vols 1–6 of *Keynsham & North Wansdyke Journal*.

Finally, we thank Mary Fairclough, Elizabeth White, Joan Day and other members of the LHS committee, as well as Bert Simpkins, David Elliot and Tony Brown for their cooperation and help with this project.